LUMBERJACK CREATURES OF THE NORTHWOODS

LUMBERJACK CREATURES OF THE NORTHWOODS

By
Chad Lewis

On the Road Publications

ISBN-10: 1733802630
ISBN-13: 978-1733802635

Printed in the United States by Documation
www.backroadslore.com

Cover Design: Rick Fisk
Artwork by Rick Fisk

Dedication

Dedicated to William T. Cox—who deserves immense credit for keeping the legends of these creatures alive and well for future generations to enjoy.

Table of Contents

Acknowledgments

First and foremost, I have to thank Minnesota Forester William T. Cox, whose 1910 book put these fearsome creatures on the map. Much of what is known about these legends can be directly tied to Cox.

Of course this book would not exist without the thousands of hard-working lumberjacks who spent their lives creating and nurturing these magnificent animals.

I also owe a lot of thanks to my hometown of Eau Claire, Wisconsin, (Sawdust City) which planted the lumberjack seed in me at an early age. Little did I know that all these years later, that little seed would grow into this book.

Like any modern researcher, I am eternally grateful for the folklorists, scholars, researchers, and authors who greatly contributed to the legends and lore of the lumberjacks including: Charles E. Brown, Dorothy Moulding Brown, Esther Shephard, Michael Edmunds, Walter Wyman, Henry Tryon, Art Childs, Eugene Shepard, and James Stevens.

All of the amazing illustrations in this guide were created by the wonderful work of Rick Fisk. Thank you for dealing with my ever-changing ideas.

Acknowledgments

A big thank you to Jerry Hajewski for lending his expertise to this book. And to Terry Fisk for loaning his skills to the creation of this book.

I must give thanks to my family which eventually scattered from the cold of the Northwoods and made their way to Florida. To my mother Judy, Todd, Kathleen, Nate, and my late nephew Sean, I am glad that you never again have to worry about encountering a snow snake!

As always, I send my love to my very own odd creatures of the Northwoods-- Nisa Giaquinto and Leo Lewis. You both would make any lumberjack want to leave the woods and come home.

Author Note

Lumberjacks believed in a vast number of puzzling animals. As of today, researchers have documented over 100 of these unusual creature legends. I have hand-picked twenty of the most bizarre, intriguing, and fascinating creatures ever said to roam the Northwoods of America. I present them here with a wink and nudge as to their credulity.

It should be specified that these lumberjack creatures are not to be confused with the study of other unknown animals like Bigfoot, sea serpents, werewolves, etc…which fall into the category of Cryptozoology. Lumberjack creatures are an entirely unique group of legends complete with their own folklore, tall-tales, and outlandish yarns.

1
The Lumberjack Era

Beginning in the mid-1800s thousands of men throughout the country left their families, farms, and hometowns in order to spend the winter up in the Northwoods cutting trees. Logging was done during the winter months for several key reasons. First, the cold weather cut down on all the bloodthirsty mosquitoes, wood ticks, and pesky insects that plagued the big woods. The ice and snow also provided the perfect conditions on the tote-roads for hauling timber. The slickness of the roads made it much easier for the horses and oxen to pull the heavy sleighs down to the river's edge. In the spring, the melting snow raised the rivers high enough that all the previously cut logs could be floated downriver to the numerous sawmills that littered every river town. After the season, most of the men would return home with a pocket full of cash to help support the family farm. Others decided to head to the first rambunctious river town they could find—These towns were only all too happy to separate the lumberjack from his hard-earned wages.

The Work—Being a lumberjack was the most physically demanding job a man could engage in. They worked six days a week with their only day off being Sunday, which was used to mend their tools or perhaps to wash the bedbugs from their clothes. Visitors were normally not allowed at camp, yet if they were, it would only be on a Sunday. The work days were brutally long. The lumberjacks often worked from can't see to can't see —-meaning that they started work before sunrise and did not finish until long after sunset. At night they would retreat to the bunkhouse to rest, dry out their wet clothing, and engage in the unofficial competition of who could tell the best tall-tales.

The Storytelling -A great number of lumberjacks were especially skilled in the fine art of storytelling. Usually a lumberjack would share a personal story—perhaps recounting the time they logged with Paul Bunyan, or boasting of their strength, cleverness, or daring, only to have another lumberjack interject with an ever more fanciful story about a wild monster in the forest. This went on and on until all the new lumberjacks were sufficiently scared and everyone got some shut eye and dreamt about the fearsome creatures lurking in the woods.

The Food- Nothing was more important to a lumberjack than the camp food. Regardless of the working conditions, the pay, the cleanliness of the bunkhouse, if the camp had a terrible cook, lumberjacks would move on to another operation. In order to fuel their exhausting work, lumberjacks had to eat as much food as they possibly could. This was also the reason that no talking was allowed at the breakfast table—-because if you were talking, you weren't eating. Supplemented with an endless amount of coffee and chewing tobacco, lumberjacks consumed a mind-boggling number of calories in three hearty meals.

The Danger - Being a lumberjack was the most dangerous career in the United States. Working with huge saws, axes, and 100-foot trees resulted in non-stop accidents and death. If the wound wasn't too severe, the men would simply plug it up with tobacco and wait until they were back at camp to have someone sew them up. Many lumber men who died at camp were buried between two pieces of bark, or if they were lucky, two large strips of wood would serve as a make-shift coffin. Those who drowned along the river would have their boots nailed to a tree as a remembrance. Every year countless men did not return from their lumber adventure.

II.
The Creatures

These are the most terrifying creatures that the lumberjacks could ever imagine. After an extremely long and exhausting day of cutting trees, the lumberjacks would retreat to their bunkhouse for a precious few hours before sleep overtook them. As the winds blew and the snow howled outside in the pitch-black darkness, the lumberjacks would sit in their bunks, smoke their pipes, and tell tall-tales to the greenhorns (young rookies). These fanciful yarns were meant to scare, warn, initiate, and entertain the new workers in the camps. The big woods of the north seemed inexhaustible, a never-ending sprawl of dense forest where anything was not just possible, but probable. The gullibility of new arrivals at the lumber camps provided the more seasoned (and mischievous) lumberjacks with an endless canvas to create mysterious creatures.

At the time, being a lumberjack was the most dangerous occupation in the country. Not only did the men have to avoid the perils of giant falling trees and swinging axes, they had to use all their smarts and cunning to avoid the numerous treacherous creatures that were said to lurk in the thick dark woods that surrounded them.

Starting in the late 1800s, folklorists and lumbermen started collecting stories of these fanciful creatures. Deadly tales of lumberjacks being attacked by these monsters, or worse, disappearing without a trace, captivated the masses, many of whom were ambivalent as to whether or not these creatures actually existed. Luckily, as evidenced by the dramatically lower number of people that go missing in modern times, many of these creatures are thought to be extinct. What was once a daily occurrence of lumberjacks getting carried off by these creatures has slowed to just a trickle.

Today, the life and work of the old lumberjacks is all but forgotten, and with this erosion of history comes the disappearance of the weird assortment of mysterious beings that now only seem to exist in our fading memories, spooky tales told around a glowing campfire. Yet, I firmly believe that as long as there are people who view the Northwoods with child-like wonder and amazement, these exotic creatures will never truly die out.

Creature 1
The Agropelter

There is no denying that the lumber industry provided numerous economic and societal benefits to the country. The lumber camps created good paying jobs for the lumbermen in the woods and in the sawmills, lumber and shingles to construct our homes, extra wood to make an assortment of farming tools, brooms, and furniture. However, with all the prosperity and convenience associated with the lumber days, we tend to overlook the devastating impact that clear cutting the forests had on the lumberjack creatures that made their home in the big woods. If we view things from the perspective of the inhabitants of the forest, we begin to see how the never-ending encroachment of humans and the swift and dreadful destruction of the woods could leave the creatures with a sour taste in their mouths. None of these creatures were more resentful of humans than the vindictive and deadly Agropelter, whose hatred for humans was unmatched in the big woods.

In appearance, the Agropelter resembles a small ape-like being. It has a slender hairy body with disproportionately long arms which William Cox described as being "muscular whiplashes." Its ape-like face is permanently locked in anger. Henry Tryon wrote that the beast's "ugly disposition is attributed in part to its diet of Hoot-owls, High-holes, and dozy wood." Others believed that the Agropelter's hunting of humans was done merely for fun and to serve as revenge as evidenced in a *Spokesman Review* article touting their dastardly character, claiming, "herbivorous by nature, the Agropelter preyed on humans for sport." To provide some cautionary advice, and perhaps to save lives, the newspaper also exposed one of the creature's favorite hunting methods: "It would hide in hollow logs, holding a bare limb as if it were an extension of a dead tree." When an oblivious hiker or lumberman passed by, the monster would swing out its long arm and hit the person with a thick tree branch. The attack was executed with such brutal force that practically no one survived the attack. It seems that the creature's anger also fueled its creativity because as more and more downed logs began being removed from the woods, the Agropelter took to perching in the tops of hollowed out trees. As most people exploring the forest set their eyes to the ground in order to avoid tripping and falling, the Agropelter, high up in the tree, was all but invisible to any wandering lumberjack or hiker. Dr. Walter Wyman discussed the sinister hunter in an interview with the *Chicago Tribune,* stating "the Agropelter is said to have waited for hours in trees for the wicked lumberjack who was devastating the forest with his axes and crosscut saws. As the woodman got close, the wiry Agropelter would clobber him with a dead branch or limb."

In her *Hawkeye History* newspaper column Martha Jordan Soland claimed the Agropelter was "perhaps the most feared creature of the lumberwoods. It threatened the lives of lumberjacks from Maine in the East to the forest of Oregon in the West." In a 1924 article, the *Kansas Star* warned that the Agropelter "is a tough customer and no woodsman hankers to meet one." The *Longview Daily News* told that "many a lumberjack has been killed by a dead branch aimed by the deadly accurate Agropelter."

Like many of these lumberjack creatures, the Agropelter has been surviving in the Northwoods for a very long time. The above-mentioned *Spokesman Review* article touched on the beast's long history, claiming that an Agropelter was "rumored to have killed a scout with the Lewis and Clark expedition." Having no known predators, for many decades the Agropelter population went unchecked, resulting in the loss of many lumberjacks. Eventually, many frightened and fed-up northwest foresters took action by forming the "Organization United to Clear the Hinterlands (OUCH) to deal with the problem." The group tried a plethora of tactics to rid the forests of the Agropelter, including, "propping up dummies in the woods dressed in logger's pants and caulked boots." Apparently the Agropelter was too smart to fall for the ruse, as it seemingly knew that the dummies posed no threat to their habitat.

The downfall of the Agropelter came not at the hands of increased hunting or more ingenious trapping methods, but by the improved management and care of the forests. As a form of fire prevention more and more hollow trees were removed from the woods, forcing the Agropelter to continuously move from forest to forest in search of new habitat and prey. Today, the Agropelter is thought to be severely endangered, if not extinct, but do not let this fact keep you from cautiously scouring the woods in search of hollow trees.

Creature 2
The Furry Trout & Other Odd Fish

In order to survive and flourish in the Northwoods, many species have to adjust to the extreme harshness of winter. While a few creatures, like the Snow Snake and Snow Wasset, actually thrive in the dreadful conditions, the insanely cold temperatures and relentless battering from blizzards challenge even the most adaptable animals. Creatures either find ways to acclimate to the brutal winters or they perish. Perhaps the greatest transformation comes in the form of the Furry Trout. The Furry Trout is nearly identical to its southern trout cousins except for the amazing fact that it has grown a thick coat of fur to insulate it from the chilled waters of the north.

It is not known when these remarkable animals first began changing from an ordinary trout to that of the fur bearing variety. A 1938 article in the *Hammond Times* claimed that "Tales of the furry fin-flippers have circulated here since Zebulon Pike first glimpsed the Rocky Mountains."

According to a 1936 article in the *Winona Republican,* Fred Kranhold, a Wisconsin fisherman, "had produced the furry trout of the Latin genus 'furre piscis,'" which had caught Minnesota anglers off guard, even though no photographic evidence was produced.

In 1938, the town of Salida, Colorado, announced its belief that the furry trout had once swum in their rivers. In an attempt to explain the marked decrease of Furry Trout sightings, the paper opined that perhaps the trout "were mistaken for beavers and exterminated by trappers," or "whether the flow of hot springs into the river has caused them to shed their fur. If there are any left, they're not as fur bearing as they were." Perhaps the real reason furry trout were so elusive came from the *Harve Daily News* which told an old tale that in Colorado the furry trout "can only be caught in January—when fishing is not permitted in Colorado's streams."

Lumberjack Creatures of the Northwoods

There seems to be something about the genetic makeup of the trout that makes it different from other fish. Over the years, researchers have discovered several other trout mutations that illustrate the creature's uncanny ability to adapt to its environment.

The Upland Trout started off like any other northern fish, that is, until it tasted its first mosquito. From then on, the pesky mosquito was the only thing the trout would eat. It spent its days and nights jumping out of the water to snatch the delicious little blood suckers.

In no time at all, the trout was spending more time soaring out of the water than it was swimming in the water. Year after year, the flying trout's fins began to grow out like wings, allowing it to fly through the air in search of food. Eventually the fish became more comfortable living out of the water. According to the *Leader Telegram,* "It built its nests in trees and flew up and down the rivers at night catching mosquitoes."

The wonderful book, *A Field Guide to Legendary Northwoods Animals* tells of the Antlered Brown Trout whose voracious appetite forced it to continually expand its feeding preferences. As the trout continued to grow bigger and bigger, frogs, minnows, and small bugs did little to quell its hunger so it began to move on to bigger game. Soon otters, muskrats, and beavers became a delicacy for the trout. However, the trout's expanding diet did not come without some unexpected consequences. Consuming so many mammals and their bones gave the trout an overabundance of calcium, which in turn caused the fish to grow giant antlers on its head. This unique mutation caught the attention of both hunters and anglers who saw the animal as the ultimate trophy. Those who possess both a deer hunting permit and a fishing license are welcome to try their hand at catching an Antlered Brown Trout, but please keep in mind that as a mammal, you might be on the Antlered Brown Trout's menu as well.

Creature 3
Sport—the Reversible Dog

Many people are unaware that Babe the Blue Ox was not the only animal friend of Paul Bunyan. Paul also had another beloved companion, his wonderful dog Sport. Arriving in camp as the tiniest of creatures, Sport almost didn't survive his first few days as a lumber dog. One night while in the darkness of the bunkhouse Paul saw what he thought was a small mouse scurrying about. Every lumberjack knew that mice could not be tolerated in their living quarters, so Paul threw his axe at the creature and cut it into two. As Paul retrieved his axe, he realized his grave mistake; what he thought was a small mouse was actually Sport the Dog. Thinking quickly, Paul grabbed the two ends of Sport and tied them back together with a burlap sack. Slowly Sport began to heal, and a couple weeks later, as Paul was removing the bandages, he noticed that in his haste, he had mistakenly attached the back half of Sport upside down so that the dog's hind legs were facing toward the sky.

Luckily Paul's unfortunate error turned out to be blessing in disguise as evidenced by the 1937 article in the *Wisconsin State Journal* that claimed Paul's mistake "proved to be all the better, because Sport could run for a while on his front legs and then reverse himself and run on his hind legs, and in this way he never got tired." Instead of acting as a hindrance, Sport's unique body helped him become the best hunting dog the world has ever seen. In 1932, the *Jefferson City Post* declared that Sport "never got tired and anything he started after got caught." When his front legs tired, he simply flipped over and used his hind legs. This constant flipping meant that there was no game that Sport could not run down.

Word of Sport's never-ending endurance and hunting prowess began to spread from lumber camp to lumber camp. In no time at all, Sport found himself as the most famous dog in the country. Soon outlandish tall tales about Sport were being featured in newspapers around the country. The *Daily Capital News* told gullible readers that Sport was "part wolf and part elephant and was raised on bear milk." For his part, Sport took his new found fame in stride, and remained one of Paul's most trusted companions. When speaking of

Sport, *The Province Sun* wrote, "Among his pets, it is said that there is one whom Paul loved very dearly. This was Sport, the Reversible Dog."

Sport was a master at using his distinctive body to his advantage and it was said that he lived a long and happy life. Sport and his female companion had many litters of puppies. Some say that to this very day, Sport's offspring can still be spotted endlessly running throughout the Northwoods. The next time you spot a dog around town, you may want to make sure that all four legs are facing the same direction.

Creature 4
The TeaKettler

On quiet nights, if you listen closely, you can hear the unmistakable sounds coming from some of the most iconic Northwoods animals. The majestic howl of the wolf, the haunting call of the loon, the raspy bellow of the moose, and the loud hissing of the Teakettler. If you are not an old-timer lumberjack you are probably wondering what the heck the Teakettler is. Don't worry if you have never heard of it, as it is one of the least known of all the lumberjack creatures. Many of the most experienced campers, who have spent their entire lives in the forest, have never laid eyes on one of these terrifically odd animals.

Perhaps one contributing factor to the lack of known Teakettler sightings stems from the creature's downright ordinary appearance, ordinary at least when compared to the rest of the beasts in this book. Shaped partly like a dog with more cat-like ears, those who are lucky enough to catch a quick glance of the Teakettler might easily mistake it for a wild dog or wolf roaming the big woods. The only notable difference is that the Teakettler is said to always walk backwards.

Although it might be quite easy to be fooled by its physical appearance, there is no mistaking the sound of a Teakettler. The animal can be heard making powerful noises like a boiling teapot letting off steam. Using its mouth as a loud whistle, it releases a high pitch screech that echoes throughout the forest. Not only does it have the uncanny ability to accurately produce the sounds of a scorching tea kettle, according to the *Dayton Daily News*, it also "issues great clouds of vapor from its head," a steam that the *Iowa City Daily* described as "vaporous clouds." The Teakettler's boiling noise is so unsettling that once it got steaming late at night, it could wake even the most exhausted lumberjack from a deep sleep.

Due to its phenomenal elusiveness, very few additional details are known about the Teakettler. Having so little information on the creature forces us to speculate on the true purpose of its weird behavior. Several leading theorists contend that the steaming is possibly used

as a mating call, or perhaps to mark its territory from other Teaket-
tlers. Maybe the strange kettle sound serves as a warning to anyone
or anything that is getting too close. It is also conceivable that the
Teakettler simply finds enjoyment and pleasure from releasing
stream as though it is singing or laughing. Of course, this is all
merely speculation and until we have more documentation of this
animal, all we can do is to keep quiet and listen for the tell-tale sign
that a Teakettler is nearby.

Creature 5
The Hugag

You should have no trouble spotting the Hugag in the woods as it is a huge animal. If you had to compare it to some common animal, the most likely comparison would be to that of a moose. However, the Hugag has many easily distinguishable physical characteristics that make any misidentification nearly impossible. A sort of hodge-podge of lumberjack creatures. Its mouth and lips are so long that they nearly touch the forest floor. Its neck and head are completely hairless and resemble sun-dried leather, while the rest of its body and tail is covered in long shaggy hair. Pine needles and sap provide an exterior shell over the beast giving it the odd appearance of some prehistoric monster. The hugag is frequently regarded as one of the most sluggish, ungainly, and dim-witted creatures to inhabit the Northwoods. The *Spokesman Review* wrote that Hugags are "Without a doubt the clumsiest, dumbest, and sweetest animals to road aspen forests."

Perhaps the most unusual part of the Hugag comes from the fact that it possesses no knee joints and therefore it is unable to bend its long legs. The resounding noise of it goose-stepping through the woods can be heard for miles. According to William T. Cox's 1910 book, *Fearsome Creatures of the Lumberwoods,* the Hugag "has a perfect mania for traveling, and few hunters who have taken up its trail ever came up with the beast." Since the beast cannot bend its legs, it has to remain standing upright at all times, even when it sleeps. To accomplish this, the clever hugag simply leans its hefty body up against a sturdy tree in order to steady itself for its nighttime slumber. In 1937, *The Providence* printed a highly entertaining article on the hugag, featuring, in part, its weird sleeping habits. Apparently "for some unexplained reason the animal always leaned against the north side of a tree, and as the years went by, countless hugags leaned against countless trees, the whole forest leaned to the south."

The adaptation of its lips prohibited the creature from simply dragging them along the forest floor scooping up food as this would
cause it to continuously step on itself. Instead, the hugag had a ten-
dency to clamp its lips tightly around the trunks of trees and strip
off their bark and pine needles.

Since practically no one was able to keep up with the surprisingly
swift and agile Hugag, lumberjacks had to implement cleverer tactics if they wanted to capture one. Knowing that the Hugag spent
its nights sleeping peacefully propped against a tree, the lumberjacks would make a deep notch in the bottom of the forest trees so
that the tree was just about to fall over. Then, when night fell and
the giant Hugag prepared for slumber, it would lean against the
flimsy tree and both the tree and hugag would come crashing down
to the ground. Once it was on the forest floor the hugag was helpless
and unable to get back up on its own. If it was not aided to its feet
by a passing lumberjack, a hugag would starve to death, or worse,
get eaten by a hungry Splinter Cat or Hodag. As detailed in the
book, *Return of the Fearsome Critters,* Paul Bunyan once used the
notched tree trick to help rid North Dakota of its huge herd of hugags. Oftentimes, the sight of so many downed trees throughout a
forest led to the erroneous belief that a tornado had ravaged the land.

Even though the Hugag's appearance may have been intimidating
and threatening, it seemed to be a gentle and unassuming creature.
In 1924, the *Kansas Star* told that the Hugag was "perfectly harm-

less and spends its time going from place-to-place stripping bark and leaves from trees." In 1976, an article in the *Dunn County News* took a playful look at some of the Hugag's favorite activities, writing, "Mostly the Hugag loved to sniff the flowers and splash in the lake and it wasn't uncommon for loggers to adopt them as pets." This docile portrayal seems inconsistent with the idea that the Hugag was a master at eluding hunters. Even more interesting was the assertion that perhaps Babe the Blue Ox was actually a member of the Hugag species, a theory that I do not ascribe to.

Today, the Hugag is thought to be long extinct. One account tells of them having died out in the northwest during the 1930s, while the *Spokesman Review* claimed that during the terrible storm of 1936, "hugags were toppled by winds and starved to death when they couldn't right themselves." It is believed that the very last of the species was killed many years ago in Turtle River, Minnesota. William Cox claimed that the last of its kind was "a young one weighing 1,800 pounds" that had gotten stuck in some thick mud. Unable to free itself, the Hugag was a sitting duck for a local hunter who ended its life. Others are not quite ready to write off the Hugag, pointing to the abundance of downed trees in the woods as evidence of the Hugag's continued existence.

Creature 6
The Snow Wasset

The Snow Wasset is the most proficient and voracious hunter the Northwoods has ever produced. On any given day it would eat a wide assortment of varmints, including: grouse, rabbits, fox, raccoons, and the occasional lumberjack. Thought to have been stranded in the north when the glaciers retreated during the last ice age, the creature has seamlessly adapted to the harsh conditions of its environment.

The best physical description of the Snow Wasset came from the *Spokesman Review,* which claimed it had a "head and fur like a polar bear and a body like a sea lion." The *Kansas Star* said it looked "for all the world like a huge walrus."

One amazing trait of the Snow Wasset is the weird metamorphosis that it goes through each year. In the winter the beast is pure white, blending perfectly with the bright snow. Its legless body allows it to stealthily slide under the snow like a seal where it sneaks up on its oblivious prey. With the spring warming, the Snow Wasset spouts rudimentary legs and is able to awkwardly amble about in the shade. Its fur takes on a dark forest green coloration that helps camouflage it from any hungry predators. The Wasset likes to estivate (hibernate) during the warmest months when its fur turns green and it finds wet moss or cranberry marsh to settle down in. In 1910, William Cox documented what happened after every first snowstorm of the season, writing, "The wasset sheds it legs and starts south, dipping about in the snow. It soon attains remarkable skill in this method of travel." In 1924, the *Kansas Star* provided a fascinating overview of the Wasset's hunting ability, writing, "It hunts by lying under a snowbank, and when it hears something passing over its head it reaches out and pulls it down under the surface." Apparently, not even wolves and bears were safe from the Wasset. This hunting prowess was echoed by the *Montana Standard*, which wrote of the huge number of "poorly adapted animals and woodsmen" that fell victim to the Wasset.

Legend tells that Native Americans and the early pioneers favored the Wasset because its legless pelt provided the perfect covering for one-man canoes. As you can imagine from its nearly perfect concealment in the snow, hunting the Wasset was nearly impossible. Even if you set a trigger wire for it, you would have no idea as to which direction its body may extend. The most successful hunters planned for this and used a dead-fall trap; once the trap line was triggered, huge logs would fall down from every direction. Even the most carefully planned and ingeniously constructed traps often failed to catch the elusive Wasset. In all the years of the Wasset inhabiting the Northwoods, there was only one in which the hunter and trapper were on an even playing field with the Wasset. That was back during the winter of the blue snow (see Babe the Blue Ox) when the Wasset's pure white coloring glowed bright against the blue snow, giving the hunters their best chance of catching the elusive Wasset. According to the *Calgary Herald*, it was during that one winter when the Wasset was "hunted to the point of decimation."

For those of you enjoying the Northwoods in the spring, summer, or fall, you have absolutely nothing to fear from the Wasset. However, if you are partaking in the plethora of winter activities that the Northwoods offers, you best hope for another winter of blue snow!

Creature 7
The Tote-Road Shagamaw

The Tote-Road Shagamaw is perhaps the most bizarre and puzzling creature of the Northwoods. Even the most seasoned hikers, hunters, and lumberjacks are unable to explain its odd behavior. Early hunters often discovered the prints of what appeared to be a bear roaming the big woods. Excited at the thrill of the chase, the hunters would follow the prints for a while when all of a sudden, the tracks changed to the distinctive hooves of a moose. Confused by the abrupt switching of animals, the perplexed hunters would continue on the path of the new tracks for a while only to discover the prints suddenly changed back to those of a bear. For years, hunters and trappers tried in vain to explain away this seemingly unnatural anomaly. Old timers suggested that perhaps a moose had befriended a bear and they were wandering the woods together, yet this explanation still could not account for the fact that only one set of tracks was found, even if those tracks represented two separate animals. The saga of the mysterious tracks would have lasted forever if not for the dogged perseverance of a determined hunter.

In his 1910 book, *Fearsome Creatures of the Lumberwoods*, Minnesota state forester William T. Cox included the first known eyewitness sighting of the elusive Tote-Road Shagamaw, writing about a hunter in Maine that, "came upon what he recognized as the tracks of a moose. After following it for about 80 rods it changed abruptly into unmistakable bear tracks: another 80 rods and it changed to moose tracks again." Through a small clearing in the thick woods the hunter spotted the weirdest animal he had ever seen. The unknown beast looked to be around 300 pounds and stood upright on its hind legs which were shaped like those of a moose. As the hunter watched in silent amazement, the creature gracefully inverted itself and began walking on its front feet which were identical to those of a bear. It appeared as though the creature would walk on its hind legs until it was worn-out and then it would switch to front legs and continue on. This constant switching ensured that it never truly tired, which also made it nearly impossible to keep up with. With the close observation of this hodgepodge creature, one of the forest's most baffling mysteries was solved, and the Tote-Road Shagamaw was officially discovered. In the years that followed the first sighting, several other lucky witnesses caught a glimpse of the curious creature and slowly more details of its appearance began to trickle in. In 1921, *The Daily Times* reported that the Shagamaw's "shoulders are like those of buffalo," and that "the rough hair of the shoulders gives way to a soft monkey fur in the middle of the back." In 1924, the *Pawnee Courier* described the Shagamaw as a "cross between a gorilla and a lion." The *Pittsburg Sun* described its odd head as being "a cross between a cow and an ape."

Today, the prevailing thought is that the Shagamaw sneakily walks the old tote-roads (unpaved roads that were used to haul supplies to the lumber camps) looking to steal any camping gear, food, supplies, or clothing which was left out by its careless owner. However, just because some intrepid woodsmen/women were lucky enough to spot the unusual creature, it doesn't mean you will have an easy time finding it. Many newspapers, including the *County Democrat,* touted the beast as being "shy and harmless." In 1941, the *Escanaba Daily Press* called it "very shy and never seen," and proclaimed that it was "impossible to track down."

Thankfully, the Shagamaw doesn't seem to pose any physical threat to humans. In 1921, the *Pittsburg Press* calmed the frazzled nerves of many outdoor-loving citizens by writing, "Nothing is known regarding the food of the animal, but the theory advanced by lumbermen is that it must feed on roots and herbs, and is harmless. It has never been known to attack any wayfarers."

Apparently the Shagamaw is more of an expert thief than a predator. So, if you happen to stumble upon any odd tracks in the woods, there is no need to panic, although it might be best to keep a close eye on your belongings.

Creature 8
The Goofus Bird
(The Filla-Ma-Loo)

Researchers estimate that there are well over 10,000 different species of birds found throughout the world, and none is more bizarre than the Goofus. Based on its unique nest building skills, weird flying preferences, and extremely odd appearance, it is easy to see why the exceptional Goofus bird is truly one of a kind.

Let's take a closer look into this rare bird to see what makes it so unique:

It has a very unusual appearance—In his *Fearsome Critters* book, Henry Tryon claimed that the Goofus had a "turkey-like head on a long bottle-green neck sparsely spangled with large, silvery scales, a black right wing and a pink left one." In 1932 the *Decatur Daily Review* went ever further, saying that it "looks like a creature from the pages of 'Alice in Wonderland.'" Such abnormally peculiar physical characteristics make spotting and identifying the Goofus bird quite easy.

The Goofus prefers to fly backwards—Outside of hummingbirds, who are able to fly backwards, hover in place, and fly upside down, no other known bird can fly backwards for any length of time. This trait is so uncommon that it makes one wonder that even if they could, why in the heck any bird would choose to fly in this manner. The answer to this question might be just as puzzling as the Goofus bird itself. One old-timer woodsman told folklorist Charles E. Brown that the Goofus flies backwards because "it doesn't give a darn where it's going, it only wants to know where it's been." Fearsome creature expert Walter Wyman claimed that the ones inhabiting Maine "fly backwards simply to keep the wind out of their faces." In 1931 the *Fort Collins Express Courier* claimed that "it thrives on a diet of chili. This makes it necessary to fly backwards keeping himself cool." The simplest explanation may have come from the *Capital Times* which speculated that "maybe they just like to do silly things all the time."

It builds its nests upside down- One of the easiest ways to spot a Goofus bird is to wander the forest in search of any nests that are hanging upside-down. At first thought, the idea of constructing a nest upside down defies gravity and makes absolutely no sense at all. How do the eggs stay in the nest? Do the birds hang upside down on the nest like a cave bat? How does the nest itself not fall to the ground? Is it attached like a bee hive? What I have learned after my many years of researching these lumberjack creatures is that these animals lie outside the realm of normal—- their habits and behavior rarely ever follow logic, reason, or science. Using this knowledge, the upside down nest turns out to be the perfect fit for the world's most unconventional bird.

The odd eccentricities of the Goofus bird are often explained away by researchers who consistently claim that the Goofus bird is of very low intelligence. However, I feel this is grossly unfair to the Goofus and an oversimplification of its albeit strange habits. I am of the firm belief that the Goofus is a truly smart and creative bird that simply likes to do things a bit differently than everyone else. Even so, it might not be advisable for you to walk backwards on your hike!

Creature 9
Babe the Blue Ox

While nearly everyone is familiar with Paul Bunyan's gigantic blue best friend, not many are aware of how Paul and Babe actually met. It happened during the winter of the blue snow. A winter that produced such severe freezing temperatures that people cursed a blue streak for so long that it turned the snow from white to blue. It was so cold—how cold was it? —it was so cold that at night when you were talking, your words froze in the air and you had to wait for the morning sunrise to thaw out the words so you could hear what your friend was saying. It was during the winter of the blue snow when Paul was making his rounds through camp that he discovered Babe stuck in the snow, frozen stiff like a board. Babe, who began life as a normal white calf, had been out in the elements so long his skin had turned blue. Paul immediately took him inside to recover, and like everything around Paul Bunyan, Babe grew to an enormous size— and he kept his blue coloring.

Paul and Babe were responsible for creating much of America's landscape. Dragging his axe behind him as he walked, Paul dug out the Grand Canyon. Paul and Babe's massive footprints created Minnesota's 10,000 lakes, and the Dakotas are mostly devoid of trees because of the logging prowess of the twosome. One day while Paul and Babe were hauling their water container it sprang a leak, flowed south and created the Mississippi River.

You are probably wondering…just how big is Babe? The most accurate calculation of Babe's size came from stories of those who worked with him as collected by folklorist Dorothy Moulding Brown who, in her book *What Say You of Paul,* described Babe as being "sixty hands high" and weighing "ten thousand pounds." Babe measured "seven axe-handles and a plug of Star tobacco between the eyes," and the tips of his long horns were "forty-two peavy handles apart." Such was the size of Babe that lumberjacks tied a string up between his horns and made such a long clothesline that all the camp's clothes could be hung out at the same time.

Outside of Paul, the only person who was tough enough to handle Babe was an ornery old man named Brimstone Bill. In her book *Paul Bunyan*, Esther Shepard claimed that Bill was uniquely qualified to handle Babe because when it came to swearing, Bill had no equal. Loggers said that once Bill started cussing, "he could keep goin' for a good half hour and never repeat the same word twice."

The mind-blowing number of amazing tales surrounding Babe the Blue Ox rivals those about Paul himself. Author Brian Gleeson captured several of these yarns in his book, *Paul Bunyan.* For example, if you watched Babe for five minutes you would see him grow right in front of you. Babe pulled a loaded sled so hard "he would straighten the chain that held it into a solid bar." Many of the old tote roads were a nasty series of winding twists, turns, and dangerous curves. If you saw these roads from the sky, you would think they spelled out every letter in the alphabet. Of course, these tangled roads only made hauling lumber more difficult so Paul came up with a brilliant idea—he hooked Babe up to one end of the road and told him to pull as hard as he could. Babe was so powerful he pulled out all the kinks and made the road straight as an arrow. The endless miles of extra road were used to make America's first roads.

By all accounts, Babe lived a wonderfully happy life. As an adult
bull he married Bessie the Yeller Cow. Tragically, many researchers
have told of numerous variations surrounding the death of Babe the
Blue Ox. Many even claim that he is buried atop Mosinee Hill in
Wausau, Wisconsin. But I believe that tales of Babe's death are the
biggest tall-tales of them all. We all know that Paul and Babe continue to wander the country in search of the next logging camp, and
if you try hard enough you might just be able to find them.

Creature 10
The Hide-Behind (Hidebehind)

Have you ever been out on a leisurely hike through the woods when you suddenly get the uneasy feeling that someone (or something) is watching you from behind? Perhaps you spin around a time or two hoping to find another hiker on the path, only to discover that absolutely nothing is there. The farther you go, the more unshakable the feeling that you are not alone becomes. Finally, you quicken your pace as the hike quickly loses its enjoyment. It would be all too easy to chalk up your unsettling feeling to an overly creative imagination. Yet many old-timers know the real reason behind your nervousness——the Hide-Behind!

As its name implies, the Hide-Behind is always hiding behind you. No matter where you go in the woods, the Hide-Behind will always be hiding behind you. If you quickly spin around 180 degrees, the Hide-Behind will still be behind you. Because of its superhuman ability to hide behind objects (trees, rocks, stumps etc…) it is believed that no one has ever actually seen one—-or at least no one has survived long enough to tell anyone of their sighting. It is said that the Hide-Behind is so skilled at hiding that it can hide behind itself. The vagueness of its physical appearance gave the lumberjack's mind free reign to conjure up the most terrifying version of the Hide-Behind.

Even though its unmatched stealthiness has made it the most elusive creature in the world, it was often the first creature that lumberjacks warned each other about. Folklorist Charles E. Brown described it as "a very dangerous animal." The *Green Bay Press Gazette* claimed it was "the most insidious creature" in the woods, and the *Casper Star Tribune* dubbed the Hide-Behind as "the most maddening menace in the forest." Perhaps the most cautionary account of the beast came from The *Bradenton Herald* which wrote that the Hide-Behind was a "dangerous animal believed to be the reason a number of lumberjacks turned up missing."

All of these gruesome warnings came for good reason. Lumberjacks regularly told of the Hide-Behind's sinister hunting of humans. As soon as you let your guard down, the Hide-Behind will swiftly leap from its hiding space and disembowel you, before carrying you off to its lair where it can enjoy its dinner (you) in private.

The most complete account of the Hide-Behind was provided in Henry Tryon's 1939 book, *Fearsome Critters*. Tryon included the only known description of the menacing monster, writing "a biggish beast, standing about six feet and walking erect....The pelt is long, thick and black, and the tail is carried recurved." Apparently, due to its odd look, it is nearly impossible to tell if the beast is coming or going. Tryon was also the first to tell of the monster's fiendish howl, which is said to be so scary it can literally frighten you to death.

Luckily, all hope is not lost for those who discover that the Hide-Behind is lurking nearby as many lumberjacks told that if you were quick enough, you could outrun a Hide-Behind before it had time to snatch you. Tryon also claimed that the Hide-Behind has a strong "aversion to the odor of alcohol," which undoubtedly has saved many a lumberjack and tourist.

In more modern times, the Hide-Behind has popped up several times in popular culture, appearing in both the Harry Potter and Gravity Falls series. One benefit to everyone carrying a camera with them at all times is that I am optimistic that someday someone will capture photographic evidence of the Hide-Behind. Just be sure to point your camera behind you!

Creature 11
The Splinter Cat

Deep in the heart of the frozen winter, as the loggers were gathered around the camp stove telling their nightly tall-tales, the sounds of cracking and splitting trees echoed through the bunkhouse. Those who were unacquainted with the mysteries of the big woods might simply dismiss these nocturnal noises as nothing more than trees being blown over by the howling winds or shattering under the brutal sub-zero temperatures. But seasoned lumberjacks knew better, they quickly recognized this as the work of the fearsome Splinter Cat.

Even by lumberjack standards, the splinter cat is a remarkable looking creature. Depending on its age, it is somewhere between the size of a calf and a bulldog. Long spikes poke out from its back, giving it the appearance of an overgrown mutant porcupine. In his *Yarns of the Big Woods* article, Art Childs described the creature as being "nearly as big as elephants, his light-colored hide has wide black stripes crossing his back from his head to the tip of his tail."

The most extraordinary part of the splinter cat is its amazingly hard face and head, which it uses to smash trees while it is hunting. You see, according to some versions of the tale, the Splinter Cat is said to live off of nothing but raccoons and honey. It scours the forest for hollow trees that might house a tasty beehive or gaze of raccoons. William Cox was the first to report on the cat's hunting prowess, claiming, "It climbs one tree, and from the uppermost branches bounds down and across toward the tree it wishes to destroy." With its hardened maul-like head, it is able to easily knock down trees to gather its rewards. Unfortunately for the forest, as the *Longview Daily News* reported, the Splinter Cat "is no mental giant. Instead of seeking a tree that hums like a taut wire, the big cat climbs any convenient elevation and launches himself towards the nearest tree, smashing it off." The cat will repeat this headache producing ritual over and over until it either finds its food or destroys itself in the process. One Splinter Cat died in this manner in a gully near Mt. Hood out in the Pacific Northwest, prompting locals to dub the creek "Splinter Cat Creek." Since its long spikes protect it from most predators, this self-destructive behavior is the only means that can help keep the Splinter Cat population in check.

Luckily, in 1924, *The Chat* printed some good news for the overall health of the woods when it declared that the splinter cat comes out only "at night or during heavy storms." Intense storms were common in the days of the lumberjacks and with each powerful blast of thunder or lightning, the men would say, "The splinter cat is sure to be on the hunt tonight." Fortunately, only prowling the forest during evening storms certainly limits the amount of destruction that the cat can cause. However, the annihilation of trees wasn't the cat's only mischievous act. A 1914 article in the *Ukiah Republican* told of the cat's proclivity to carry "off forks and knives from the camps," while also engaging in the theft of fire wood. Following in the footsteps of the cutlery theft was an even more unusual explanation for the cat's tree smashing. Long before Yogi Bear was stealing cartoon lunches from park visitors, the splinter cat was grabbing lunches of its own. A newspaper reader sent a letter to the *Longview Daily News* claiming that the cat lived "on lunches which they steal from hikers in the woods." Once the cat strikes a tree, "One of the splinters, which fly in every direction, will go through the clothes of the hiker, pinning him to the ground. The splinter cat can then come down and steal his lunch."

Little is known about the social habits of the splinter cat. Fortunately, in 1939, the *Hartford Courant*, published some tantalizing information about the cat from an old timer dressed in the conventional mackinaw who opined, "I have never heard of a hodag traveling with a splinter cat." As of today, researchers have been unable to figure out whether the dangerous cats hunt in packs, or if they are solitary creatures.

As lumberjacks quickly learned, trees were not the only victims of the Splinter Cat. Owing to the cat's lower intelligence it often mistook straying loggers for trees. Instead of bashing into the trunk of a tree, the cat found its target in the chest of a lumberjack. Anyone who found themselves on the receiving end of a splinter cat's head met an instant death. In the old days, the last thing many lumbermen saw was the fast-approaching head of the splinter cat.

The Splinter Cat gets let off the hook for the dastardly destruction it causes because toppled trees are almost always blamed on hurricanes, tornadoes, and heavy storms. Today, many scientists and naturalists fear that the alarming rate at which honeybees are dying off will severely impact the survival of the Splinter Cat. As you make your way through the woods, keep an eye out for any smashed trees, knowing that a splinter cat might be lurking in a tree waiting to make you its next target.

Creature 12
The Axe-Handle Hound

Many of the lumberjack creatures of the woods were terrifying, some were downright dangerous, and a few of them were even deadly, but none was more of a nuisance to the lumber camp than the dreaded Axe-Handle Hound. One might think that it would be a great benefit to have a dog in the camp, but one lone Axe-Handle Hound could put a significant damper on any camp's lumber output. The Axe-Handle Hound had an insatiable hunger that could be satisfied only by eating the wooden handle of an axe. Because of this exotic taste in food, the axe handle hound was known far and wide as the bane of lumberjack camps.

Back in 1922, Art Childs best summed up their odd appearance, writing in his national newspaper column, "It's about one and a half times as big as an axe handle and looks like its name, having a long body covered with rope colored hair, and a hatchet face with saw teeth and cross-cut eyes." *The Missoulian* claimed it was as "long as a dachshund." In his fantastic book, *Fearsome Critters*, Henry Tryon described their body as "slender and axe handle shaped, with short stumpy legs." At night, when the exhausted lumbermen were snoring away in the bunkhouse, the nocturnal Axe-Handle Hound would stealthily prowl around the camp in search of any axe handles that had been foolishly left out. Its appetite for peavey handles was legendary.

When writing about Paul Bunyan's wild animals, folklorist Charles E. Brown claimed "whole cords of axe handles were eaten by these troublesome wild hounds." The hound's endless appetite was also documented by Henry Tryon who heard that in just one evening the beast could "consume two boxes of DB handles and sixteen six-foot peavy stocks." Many lumberjacks cursed their luck as they awoke early in the morning to find their axe had been consumed by the hungry little prowler.

Even though the Axe-Handle Hounds could cause significant damage and loss for the lumber camp, they were thought to make great pets, if one could afford to feed them. Apparently, the only axe handles the hounds would not eagerly gobble down were those made from red oak. It is not known if in times of desperation or starvation the Axe-Handle Hound resorts to eating campfire wood, but you might want to keep an eye on your stock just in case!

Creature 13
The Jackalope

If you have ever stopped at a roadside tourist gift shop then you have probably seen a replica of a Jackalope for sale. Looking like some bizarre cross between a jackrabbit and an antelope, the Jackalope is one of the most widely-known and most iconic examples of the lumberjack creatures. If it weren't for its large deer-like antlers, the Jackalope might be easily mistaken for a large rabbit.

Even though the Jackalope is most commonly associated with the prairies and deserts of the Southwest, their range actually covers the entire United States. However, just because they have evolved to survive and thrive in nearly any environment, that doesn't mean they are easy to spot. In 1997, the *Pantagraph* newspaper labeled the Jackalope as "probably the rarest animal in North America." The fact that they are nocturnal only adds to their elusiveness as evidenced by the *Casper Star Tribune,* which wrote, "It is nearly impossible to spot one of these nocturnal animals at night...its lightning-like speed (up to 90 mph when motivated) makes it even harder to visualize, causing even the most 20/20 sighted among us to be unsure of exactly what flashed by." It is not uncommon for Jackalopes to cover over 25 feet in a single leap and it regularly dashes across the land at speeds over 60 miles per hour. Adding to the rarity of sightings is the fact that Jackalopes are thought to be extremely shy. In an article for the *Desert Star* one researcher talked of its shyness, stating, "It is a timid creature and humiliated at laughter and ridicule—which you can easily understand its strange appearance would cause."

Luckily, there are several means by which you can attract the Jackalope. Odds are you will likely hear a Jackalope long before you actually see one. Old cowboys often told stories of sitting around a campfire at night as they relaxed from a dusty day on the range. As the cowboys took turns singing their favorite songs, they would hear a soft harmonizing voice echoing from the darkness. It is believed that Jackalopes possess an uncanny ability to imitate the human voice and love to sing old cowboy songs. Lumberjacks would hear the Jackalope singing along with the rhythm of the swinging axe and the humming of the crosscut saws.

One sure-fire means of attracting the Jackalope is to sing old songs like "Home on the Range," or "Get Along Little Doggies" as you sit around the campfire. After a few renditions of these cowboy classics, you might get lucky and catch a glimpse of one hiding on the outskirts of the fire's flickering flames.

For decades, people have been using alcoholic beverages to lure in Jackalopes. The most effective spirit seems to be whiskey. The *Casper Star Tribune* elaborated on this technique, claiming that old time trappers would "lure them with alcoholic beverages. The bait made them giddy to the point where they dared each other to catch bullets with their mouths." Apparently, the temptation of the drink was so seductive to the Jackalope it was deemed too unfair of a hunting advantage, and the baiting practice was outlawed. The heavy scent of beer and liquor is so powerful that it can attract Jackalopes from miles away. However, unlike stubborn lumberjacks, the Jackalope has learned its lesson from the ill effects of alcohol and swore it off. Even though it still loves the smell, it no longer imbibes any spirits.

The question that continues to baffle most naturalists and scientists is "Where did these creatures come from?" Was it some freak genetic mutation, or the demented creation of a mad scientist? According to the book, *The Field Guide to North American Jackalope*, no one is really sure, although it is theorized that they originated in Asia. The Douglas (Wyoming) Area Chamber of Commerce claims that in 1829 a trapper named Ray Ball was the first person to spot the weird creature—-and they should know as Douglas is known as the "Jackalope Capital of the World."

Some scientists who are not well versed with lumberjack creatures contend that Jackalopes are nothing more than everyday hares that are suffering from Shope Papilloma Virus (SPV), which is a virus that causes horn-like warts to form on the head, neck, and shoulders of rabbits. Yet, even the most inebriated cowboy can tell the difference between a Jackalope and common SPV infected cottontail.

Legend states that unlike its cousin, the rapidly reproducing cottontail, the Jackalope only mates during stormy nights, particularly during extreme thunderstorms, where heavy cloud cover affords them some privacy. Perhaps as a conflation with the idea of a rabbit's foot being lucky, many people regard seeing the Jackalope as a sign of good luck being in your future. All that is left to do is to gather your family around a campfire, grab your guitar, and begin luring in the Jackalope.

Creature 14
The Camp Chipmunk

As you can imagine, lumber camps needed a tremendous amount of food to continuously fuel the lumberjacks' bottomless appetites. One of the favorite treats of the time were prunes, which were used in everything from desserts and baked treats to juices and dried snacks. The only drawback to prunes is that they have hard pits (stones) inside that need to be discarded. Several men would spend their day dumping wheelbarrow after wheelbarrow of the useless pits on the outskirts of the camp. The chipmunks in the forests mistook the hard pits for nuts and began consuming them as fast as the cook could dump them. At first, the lumberjacks thought that this was an example of recycling functioning at its best. However, the

consumption of so many prune pits had one unintended consequence that no one could have ever predicted...the chipmunks
started to grow to enormous size.

In theory, the idea of giant-sized chipmunks was not considered to
be a serious problem. At first, some of the men even considered the
overgrown beasts as cute and cuddly, but in reality, the large chipmunks were rapidly throwing off the entire ecosystem of the Northwoods. Wisconsin folklorist Charles E. Brown wrote that the
chipmunks "grew so big and fierce that they killed all of the bears
and catamounts in the neighborhood." In no time at all lumberjacks
began noticing the disappearance of wolves, deer, moose, and other
big game animals. The chipmunks had grown to such a massive size
that when spotted by the general public they were often mistaken
for vicious roaming tigers.

Fearing that they would be the next prey on the deadly chipmunks'
list, lumberjacks quickly decided that something needed to be done
in order to restore the delicate balance of the Northwoods. Hunting
parties were swiftly organized and within no time at all, the humon-
gous chipmunks were nearly completely killed off. To avoid another
resurgence of the deadly beasts, camp cooks took special care in
where they discarded the prune pits. Legends from old-timers say
that many giant chipmunks escaped the hunting parties and have
evolved to the point where they can now survive from eating all
sorts of leftover food. This fact should give you pause the next time
you look to discard your half-eaten snack in the woods.

Creature 15
The Snow Snake

Just as its name implies, the Snow Snake is a snake that hibernates all spring, summer, and fall, and only comes out after the first winter snow. Except for its pale blue eyes (some say pink) its entire body is snowy white, which makes it nearly impossible to spot because it perfectly blends in with the fresh winter snow. The true origin of the snow snake is anyone's guess. In his 1939 book *Fearsome Critters*, Henry Tryon claimed that during the year of the two winters, "these pink-eyed, white bodied savage serpents crossed over from Siberia." Others contend that they are a native inhabitant of the Northwoods, but until fairly recently, their mastery of using the snow as camouflage had just kept them undiscovered.

A newspaper report from 1920 tells of the snake being "a giant cousin of the Alaskan Ice Worm." In the same article, Minnesota's first state forester, William T. Cox, told the newspaper that the Snow Snake survives almost entirely on snowshoe hares that it voraciously hunts. It is also during this time period that saw the first varying accounts of the creature having a tufted ball-like clump of fur on its tail that it utilizes like a shovel to help propel it through the snow.

In the late 1920s and early 1930s, Art Childs wrote a series of weekly national newspaper articles under the heading of *Yarns of the Big Woods*, in which he featured many of the strange creatures of the Northwoods. In his article on the Snow Snake, Childs expanded on the creature's hunting preferences, claiming, "They are supposed to live on owls, weasels, and other birds and animals." Being so adept at stealth, it seems probable that the snake could eat whatever animals it wanted.

How to Catch a Snow Snake?

Originally, old timers told that the best way to catch a Snow Snake was to lay out a line of raisins on top of the snow to lure them out.

However, in 1954, the *High Point Enterprise* ran a fascinating story detailing the clever means which Native peoples had devised to capture the snake. Due to the snake's fondness for sweets, they would use black gum drops to discover its location. Apparently, "The snow snake hunter places a few of these tidbits on the snow" and then watches closely. Eventually, the hungry snake will make a search for hard-to-find winter food and fall for the gum drop bait. As soon as a drop disappears, a hunter can grab at the exact spot where the drop was and snatch up the snow snake. Over time it was discovered that these snakes actually enjoyed black cough drops above all other treats. However, unlike in humans, the cough drops actually caused the snake to suffer a severe coughing fit that would cause them to turn blue and become visible against the snow.

In 1960, the *Delaware County Daily Times* ran an article claiming that a local scientist had actually caught a live Snow Snake. Unfortunately, trapping a deadly unknown creature was not the wisest decision and the scientist quickly fell victim to his catch. When the authorities finally found his research journal, his notes indicated that the snake could bite from either end of its body.

How Can It Bite You?

There are several ways for lumberjacks to suffer the wrath of the Snow Snake.

1   Just like an ordinary snake, the Snow Snake can bite you, and since it is perfectly camouflaged by the bright white snow, you will probably never even see it coming. Its bite is fatal, but not because of any powerful venom; instead, if you are bitten by a snow snake you will freeze to death.

2   A more painful death comes to those who are unlucky enough to catch a glimpse of the elusive creature. Although extremely rare, when sighted, the snake will rise up and begin hissing at the startled passerby. Usually the fear-stricken witness stands frozen with fear with their mouth agape. When this happens, the snow snake will launch itself down your throat and freeze you from the inside.

3   A much lesser-known means of death comes from the belief that the Snow Snake is a constrictor. Any unfortunate woodman that wandered near the beast would be quickly wrapped up and squeezed to death by the ferocious monster.

Thankfully, science was able to find an antidote that could save the life of any unfortunate lumberjack that suffered the bite of a Snow Snake. In order to survive the bite, a lumberjack would have to consume a significant amount of booze. A 1958 article in the *Wisconsin State Journal* detailed just how much liquor it would take to cure a lumberjack, writing, "When he starts rocking around the stool and begins seeing things that aint there, he is in the clear."

Luckily, Snow Snake bites were thought to only last a couple of hours so that "by that time a feller auta be fulla tonic." Since alcohol was not allowed in most lumber camps, I wonder if any exceptions were made in order to save the life of the infected lumberjack. The late Wisconsin folklorist Charles E. Brown wrote briefly of another cure for the bite in his monograph, *Paul Bunyan Natural History.* Brown stated that tanglefoot oil was the only known remedy for the snake's bite. Being "treed" by a Snow Snake was a common explanation used by those who were scolded by their spouses for arriving home later than expected. If you are looking to use this excuse with your loved ones, please keep in mind that it only is believable during the winter months.

Creature 16
The Bee-Squito

The majority of wood cutting was done during the harsh winter months in order to avoid mosquitoes, ticks, and various other pesky bugs that plagued the warmer seasons of the year. However, every lumberjack knows that Northwoods mosquitoes are a completely different species of bloodsuckers. Not only are they gigantic, the frigid temperature does nothing to slow their insatiable blood thirst, and since lumberjacks were the only people foolish enough to be camped out in the woods during winter, they served as the winged predators' main source of food. The gargantuan mosquitoes were known to pluck even the biggest of lumberjacks right off the ground and carry him off to painful death. Soon, the lumber axes and saws were being used more to fight the ferocious insects than they were to cut lumber. Even the enclosed buildings of the lumber camp provided little protection as evidenced by a 1923 article in *The Missoulian* that told "the mosquitoes were so large and daring that they would attack the messhouse in large numbers, tear the shakes from the roof, and two or three of them would attack a man at the same time." As more and more men fell victim to the marauding blood suckers, lumberjacks decided something had be done, so they turned to the one man they trusted above all others…Paul Bunyan.

Paul was an extremely clever man and upon hearing of the deadly mosquitoes Paul quickly got to work on hatching an ingenious plan. In his long career as a lumberjack, Paul had worked in nearly every forest in the entire country. As he sought a solution for the Northwoods mosquito he quickly remembered a similar trouble he had down South with a swarm of giant bumblebees. Paul's daring plan was put into play as he sent a trusted associate down South to wrangle up a bunch of these colossal bees and bring them back to the Northwoods, where they would most certainly wage war on the dreadful mosquitoes. However, Paul's nearly perfect plan had one unintended consequence that was documented by the *Daily Advertiser,* which wrote:

When those bees met those mosquitoes, they hit it off with each other right from the start. Pretty soon they were buzzing and swinging and stinging and singing together, and then those bees began to marry those mosquitoes, and their children were really terrible because they had stingers on the front and back, and they could sting a fella coming or going.

Even worse, some of the giant bees married fireflies, giving their offspring the ability to see in the dark. The lumberjacks were now dealing with something even more monstrous than just giant mosquitoes; they now had to fear the Bee-Squito. Even the strongest, sturdiest, and bravest lumberjack stood little chance of fending off Bee-Squitos, which were armed with two huge deadly stingers. Luckily, mother nature came to the lumberjacks' rescue. The new Bee-Squito species had inherited the bees' intense hunger for sweets, which when added with the voracious appetite of the mosquito, combined to make an insect that went absolutely mad whenever any sweets or sugary items were nearby. This fatal flaw would cause their near extinction, which was covered in full detail by the *Wisconsin Rapids Daily Tribune,* which wrote, "One day the whole tribe flew across Lake Superior to attack a fleet of ships bringing sugar to Paul's camps. They destroyed the ships but ate so much sugar they could not fly and drowned."

That is the story of how the Bee-Squitos went extinct…well, not exactly. It seems the above mentioned story included some wishful thinking; in actuality, several Bee-Squitos had stayed back at camp to tend to the tribe's vast supply of honey. It is said that to this very day their offspring continue to lurk in the Northwoods endlessly searching for unsuspecting victims. Although there may be many fewer Bee-Squitos in today's world, you still might want to keep your sugary snacks safely tucked away.

Creature 17
The Side-Hill Gouger
(Side-Hill Winder; Gyascutus)

There is no more remarkable example of an animal adapting to its environment than that of the Side-Hill Gouger. If you have ever gazed up at a mountain or large hill and spotted odd trail-like paths cutting across the steep terrain, you have seen the evidence of the Side-Hill Gouger. This mountain goat sized four-legged mammal spends its entire life walking on sloped ground. From the Pacific

Northwest to the Great Lakes and over to the Northeast, the Gouger can be found in nearly every state that has a mountain or any sufficiently large hills.

But life was not easy for the early Gouger. Anytime a Gouger attempted to make a vertical climb up a hill, it always failed, forcing the species to make a series of slow spiral-like loops going up and around in search of food. In order to thrive in these uneven vertical conditions, the Side-Hill Gouger eventually evolved to the point where the legs on one side of its body began growing longer than those of the other side—a clever adaptation that allowed the Gouger to easily maneuver even the most difficult of mountains and hillsides. A 1910 article in *The Washington Post* claimed that "the animal belonged to the cat family, but was larger and more ferocious than any member of the feline tribe," and loved to devour small prey. Others paint them as a friendly, harmless, docile grazer of plants, fruits, and vegetables.

Unfortunately, the Gouger's ingenious evolution came with one major drawback—-it could only travel in one direction for its entire life. If a Gouger attempted to turn around and run in the other direction, it would lose its balance and tumble down the hill and never be able to climb back up.

In the early 1900s, naturalists, scientists, and exotic game hunters attempted to capture one of these rare creatures. In a 1920 article, the *Helena Independent* claimed that Gougers were no longer inhabiting Montana, writing, "in the early days they roamed the hills in colonies but being prized for their flesh as well their fur, like the buffalo they were hunted to extinction. In 1922, the *Edmonton Journal* published the following hunting tip for anyone looking to secure a specimen, writing "the way to catch one is to meet him face to face and hit him in the head with a club," thus spinning him around and forcing him to roll down the hill—-an act that "makes him so dizzy that he never comes to again." Six years later the *Edmonton Journal* followed up their hunting advice with a baiting technique that claimed that the Gouger is very fond of ice cream, and that hardy mountaineers found that the Gouger could "be tempted within rifle range by setting outside the cabin door the left-overs from dessert."

Amazingly, in 1931 the *Rhinelander Daily News* reported that a "side-hill gouger was captured near Florence, Wis., and arrived in a specially made box today." The live specimen was to be put on display with a Hodag that was also captured in Wisconsin.

Researchers now believe there are two distinct species of the Side-Hill Gouger, one that travels around the hill in a clockwise direction and one that moves in a counterclockwise direction. For obvious mobility issues the two species never breed with one another, and even if they did, we might not be able to witness it as many researchers claim that the Gougers turn invisible when they mate.

Regardless of whether they are harmless and friendly or ferocious and deadly, if you encounter one just make sure you know which is the best direction for you to run away.

Creature 18
The Hodag

Since the late 1800s, lumbermen, hunters, hikers, and naturalists all spoke about a hideous monster lurking in the Northwoods of America. If the eye-witnesses were to be believed, the creature was more bizarre than anything ever imagined. Described as a giant lizard with thick curved spikes flowing down its back and two thundering horns set atop its head, its four feet are equipped with razor sharp claws and its mouth is filled with deadly dagger-like teeth that can rip apart anything they come in contact with.

Although tales of the unsightly monstrosity had been circulating through the lumber camps for some years, it wasn't until the late 1880s that newspapers began bringing the legend to the masses. In 1889, there was a widely circulated article telling of a man who spotted an exhibit advertising a live Hodag. Upon paying his 25-

cent admission, the man was distraught to discover that the Hodag was sick and not on display.

In 1892, cryptic ads began appearing in newspapers across the country touting the capture of the only known Hodag, which naturalists were calling "the greatest wonder on the face of the earth." Of course, the creature was to be exhibited to the public. And just in case any skeptics might have had second thoughts about visiting the creature, the papers warned their readers not to miss it because "if you do you will regret it as long as you live."

The person most associated with the Hodag legend was a well-known timber cruiser of the Northwoods named Eugene Shepard. A life-long woodsman who moved to the Rhinelander, Wisconsin, area, Shepard was known far and wide for his expertise in the lumber industry and his fantastic story-telling skills. No other individual knew as much about the Hodag as Shepard. In an infamous 1893 article in Rhinelander's *New North* newspaper, he asserted that the Hodag "assumes the strength of the ox, the ferocity of a bear, the cunning of the fox, and the sagacity of a Hindoo snake, and is truly the most to be feared of all the animals that lumberjacks come in contact with."

The description of the Hodag was not the most amazing part of the *New North* article, as Shepard also claimed that in 1893, he and a posse of men wandered into the Northwoods to hunt the Hodag. It didn't take long for the group to encounter the vicious beast and the fight was on. The hunters felt confident as they were equipped with heavy rifles, dynamite, and several prized hunting dogs. Unfortunately, the Hodag made quick work of the dogs, tearing them to shreds before the men could put an end to the brutal killer.

In 1896, Shepard told an even more fantastical story of heading to the woods with his fellow hunters when, all of a sudden, they surprised a Hodag in its den, and after some clever thinking, and a long pole doused with chloroform, Shepard was finally able to capture a living specimen of the creature he had so desperately been seeking. Shepard promptly put it on display at local fairs and carnivals for any paying customer to see. Eventually he kept the beast in a pit in the yard at his Rhinelander home.

Where does the Hodag come from?

There are two main stories of how the Hodag came about. The first came from the same 1893 *New North* article written by Eugene Shepard who detailed the belief that "when an ox is butchered or accidentally killed in the woods, that his spirit turns into a Hodag." Oxen were often used in the lumber camps to haul the cut timber to the river banks. Due to the brutal work and deadly conditions, the oxen did not enjoy long or pleasurable lives. Add in the constant swearing and abuse that came from the lumberjacks and you can see why the spirit of the ox would be so angry.

In another old-timer lumberjack legend the Hodag was created when the lumber camps disbanded for the summer and simply left their oxen to fend on their own until the startup of logging the following fall. When the men returned to camp, they found the oxen had transformed into Hodags.

Yet, nothing in the world of lumberjack creatures is ever perfectly cut and dried. In 1897, the *Philadelphia Inquirer* printed a story about the Hodag "laying eggs," of which several were said to have been located at the bottom of its nest.

What does the Hodag eat?

Like many Northwoods animals, the Hodag was not a particularly picky eater. Snakes, rabbits, and turkeys were all fair game to this ferocious beast. In 1900, an article in the *Bemidji Pioneer* wrote "the Hodag is a meat eater, and subsides on moose and kindred game which it rushes upon and rips with its horns." However, over the years the Hodag developed a hankering for white bulldogs which quickly became its favorite delicacy.

Today the legend of the Hodag is a hotly debated issue. Skeptics claim that Shepard was nothing more than a huckster, a master hoaxer. Others contend that the Hodag, which was extremely rare even in the 1800s, went extinct many years ago. Yet for all the disbelievers, there is an equal number of those who believe that the deadly Hodag is alive and well and is still prowling the Northwoods of America and it is best for your health if you never encounter it.

Creature 19
The Hoop Snake

Those who have not spent much time in the Northwoods might naively believe that the cheetah is the fastest land animal on the planet. Yet those who have had the displeasure of being chased through the forest know all too well that the Hoop Snake is the undisputed champion of speed. At first glance the Hoop Snake appears like an ordinary snake in the woods. However, this snake has gained the amazing ability to tuck its tail into its mouth to form a hoop. As the reptile starts rolling, it picks up more and more speed. Soon it is moving so fast that author Henry Tryon called it an "engine of destruction." The *Edwardsville Intelligencer* went further and dubbed it a "speed demon."

To make matters worse, the Hoop Snake is equipped with a venomous spear-like stinger at the end of its tail, making it the world's deadliest snake as well. If anything (or anyone) is unfortunate enough to get in its path, the snake will unroll itself and pierce its stinger into the victim, causing certain death.

In 1927, the *Forest City Courier* reported on the fascinating encounter of a young woman who was being chased by the Hoop Snake, and as the snake readied itself to attack her, she darted behind a tree just as the snake's tail lodged itself into the bark. A few moments later, "part of the family went to the recent scene of hostilities. The snake was fastened to the tree and the leaves of the tree were drooping and wilting and died promptly."

There are also countless tales of the Hoop Snake striking wooden axes, rake handles, fence posts, canes, etc… only to have the object swell to an enormous size. One such tale was told to the *Kenosha News* involving an old-timer who was walking down the road when he noticed a large Hoop Snake rolling toward him. The man decided to bravely stand his ground and when the snake got close he smacked it with his peavy axe handle. The "peavy swelled and swelled until it was an enormous log. It was pulled to the sawmill by several teams of horses." Apparently, any wood infected by a Hoop Snake does not make for a good campfire as it just smokes and hisses.

If you ever find yourself being chased by a Hoop Snake, here are several surefire tips to save you:

1 The best way to escape a Hoop Snake is to climb over a fence as the snake will have to unroll in order to get through. Unfortunately, fences are sometimes hard to come by.

2 While you are being chased, if you are able to jump through the hoop of the snake, the snake will become so confused by your action that it will lose its concentration and fall to the ground.

3 The Hoop Snake is incredibly fast, especially while traveling downhill. However, when it has to travel uphill, it is a much different story. Find the steepest incline you can and the Hoop Snake will quickly run out of momentum.

4 If you happen to be in the woods you can simply climb a tree and escape the snake. However, you should be warned that this is the least effective of your choices. Hopefully, once you are in the safety of the tree, the snake will lose interest and venture off in search of other victims. But be

warned, if the Hoop Snake is especially hungry it will do one of one of two things. It will lie down beside the tree and try to wait you out or strike the tree with its poisonous tail, which could kill the tree very quickly. Either way, climbing a tree is a much safer option than foolishly trying to outrun it.

Creature 20
The Whirling Whimpus

The Whirling Whimpus has a long history of being one of the most feared creatures in the Northwoods. In 1919, the *Buffalo Evening News* told of the Whimpus being "the oldest terror which besets the 'still' hunters and other sportsman." In 1982, the *Spokesman Review* wrote "neither snakes nor alligators scared woodsmen in Arkansas, but the Whirling Whimpus made them quake in their boots." The

Central News Home claimed that the Whirling Whimpus was responsible for the untold number of deaths of "people who have gone to walk in the forest but have never returned."

With all the terror and dread surrounding this legend, you are probably wondering what in the heck makes the Whirling Whimpus so scary. Let's start with the physical descriptions that come from eyewitnesses who have spotted the beast and somehow miraculously survived to tell their tale. The Whimpus stands around seven feet tall and has a long muscular gorilla-like body that is covered in a light fur. Attached to the imposing body are two tiny hind legs, but the creature's front legs (or arms) are what you should be afraid of. In his book, *Fearsome Critters,* Henry Tryon described the beast's front legs as being "disproportionately long, sinewy and powerful." As threatening and intimidating as the Whimpus looks, its ghastly actions are infinitely more terrifying.

The Whimpus is a super carnivore, an apex predator, and a non-picky one at that. It will eagerly devour bears, deer, hogs, turkeys, lumberjacks, lost hikers, hunters, or whatever other poor soul crosses its deadly path. Its favorite means of hunting is to stealthily stand near a bend in the road and wait for any unsuspecting lone travelers to wander along. When its prospective meal gets close, the Whimpus stretches out its long burly arms and begins to rapidly whirl around on its pointy hind feet like a spinning top. As it spins faster and faster, the Whimpus reaches such incredible rates of rotation that it becomes practically invisible. The only evidence that tells you something is amiss is a soft droning noise that is produced by its whirling. The whirring noise, which sounds like it is emanating from the treetops, also has the added effect of attracting curious parties. Before the ill-fated victim can figure out the cause of the odd noise, it is already too late – and believe me, the outcome is not pretty.

The *Wausau Daily Herald* described the gory killing this way: the traveler "is immediately deposited in the form of an unctuous syrup." The *News Leader* compared it to being "chopped into hamburger." The bony outstretched arms of the beast, combined with the amazing rotating velocity, turns the Whimpus into a gigantic blender. Once it is satisfied that it has transformed its prey into pulp, the Whimpus quits spinning and wanders into the woods to enjoy the fruits of its labor. The *Calgary Herald* said the Whimpus "was able to lick its victims off its paws like so much honey." The *Associated Press* added to the gruesomeness by claiming that the Whimpus "with great relish licks off the syrup" from its huge paws and enjoys its supper.

The exact number of people who have met their gelatinous end at the literal hands of the Whirling Whimpus is not known. Every year, hundreds of people walk into the woods and never return, yet it is impossible to say which of the various lumberjack creatures is responsible for the disappearances. Just to be safe, much like when encountering a poisonous snake, experts advise that if you hear any odd whirring noises in the woods, you should immediately stop and slowly back away from the area.

Works Consulted

Agropelter

Burlington Hawk Eye. March 19, 1978.

Chicago Tribune. May 4, 1979.

Cox, William. *Fearsome Creatures of the Lumberwoods*. Judd &Detweiler. 1910.

Kansas City Star. May 2, 1924.

Longview Daily News. February 13, 1965.

Orange County Register. May 16, 1979.

Spokesman Review. April 3, 1982.

Tryon, Henry. *Fearsome Critters*. Idlewild. 1939.

Uniontown Morning Herald. July 5, 1949.

Victoria Daily Times. May 20, 1941.

Furry Trout

Hammond Times. December 9, 1938.

Havre Daily News. January 10, 1939.

Leader Telegram. September 16, 1978.

Winona Republican. May 19, 1936.

Winter, Gallen & Boettcher, John. *A Field Guide to Legendary Northwoods Animals*. Willow Creek Press. 1994.

Sport the Reversible Dog

Daily Tribune. May 19, 1934.

Jefferson City Post. September 25, 1932.

Province Sun. October 5, 1930

Wisconsin State Journal. July 21, 1937.

Teakettler

Daily Iowan. February 20,1970.

Dayton Daily News. April 24, 1981.

Hugag
Cox, William. *Fearsome Creatures of the Lumberwoods.* Judd
&Detweiler. 1910.
Dunn County News. October 20, 1976.
Kansas City Star. May 2, 1924.
Province. August 3, 1937.
Spokesman Review. April 3, 1982.
Warren, James & McQuarrie, Susan Hopkins. *Return of the
Fearsome Critters.* Your Nickel's Worth Publishing. 2008.

Snow Wasset
Calgary Herald. December 9, 1963.
Cox, William. *Fearsome Creatures of the Lumberwoods.* Judd
&Detweiler. 1910.
Kansas City Star. May 2, 1924.
Pittsburgh Press. January 4, 1944.
Spokesman Review. April 3, 1982.

Tote-Road Shagamaw
County Democrat. November 8, 1929.
Cox, William. *Fearsome Creatures of the Lumberwoods.* Judd
&Detweiler. 1910.
Daily Times. August 18, 1921.
Escanaba Daily Press. June 1, 1946.
Pawnee Courier Dispatch. May 15, 1924.
Pittsburg Sun. August 30, 1921.

Goofus Bird
Brown, Charles E. *Paul Bunyan Natural History.* Wisconsin
Historical Society. 1935.
Decatur Daily Review. July 10, 1932.

Fort Collins Express Courier. February 16, 1931.
Tryon, Henry. *Fearsome Critters*. Idlewild. 1939.

Babe the Blue Ox
Brown, Dorothy Moulding. *What Say You of Paul.* D.M. Brown. 1947.
Edmonds, Michael. *Out of the Northwoods: The Many Lives of Paul Bunyan.* Wisconsin Historical Society Press. 2009.
Gleeson, Brian & Meyerowitz, Rick. *Paul Bunyan.* Rabbit Ears Productions. 1990.
Shepard, Esther. *Paul Bunyan.* Harcourt, Brace & Company. 1943.

Hide-Behind
Bradenton Herald. April 16, 1986.
Brown, Charles E. *Paul Bunyan Natural History.* Wisconsin Historical Society. 1935.
Casper Star Tribune. December 5, 1982.
Enterprise Journal. April 30, 1937.
Green Bay Press Gazette. February 25, 1973.
Tryon, Henry. *Fearsome Critters*. Idlewild. 1939.

Splinter Cat
Atchison Daily Globe. September 11, 1924.
Cox, William. *Fearsome Creatures of the Lumberwoods.* Judd &Detweiler. 1910.
Chat. October 11, 1924.
Hartford Courant. February 26, 1939.
Kansas Star. May 2, 1924.
Longview Daily News. February 13, 1965.
Longview Daily News. February 18, 1965.
Pawnee Courier Dispatch and Times. May 15, 1924.
Ukiah Republican Press. October 30, 1914.
Wisconsin Rapids Daily Journal. September 30, 1978.

Axe-Handle Hound

Brown, Charles E. *Paul Bunyan Natural History*. Wisconsin
　　Historical Society. 1935.
Daily Telegram. September 27, 1922.
Missoulian. April 1, 1957.
Tryon, Henry. *Fearsome Critters*. Idlewild. 1939.

Jackalope

Robbins, Andy. *The Field Guide to North American Jacka-*
　　lope. Sweetgrass Books. 2019.
Casper Star Tribune. July 13, 1959.
Casper Star Tribune. April 23, 1992.
Desert Star. March 16, 1972.
Pantagraph. February 23, 1977.
Petaluma Argus Courier. March 26, 1956.
Phoenix Republic. March 26, 1967.
Tampa Bay Times. December 25, 1977.
Winona Daily News. September 29, 1972.

Camp Chipmunk

Brown, Charles E. *Paul Bunyan Natural History*. Wisconsin
　　Historical Society. 1935.

Snow Snake

Boston Globe. January 25, 1920.
Burlington Hawk Eye. May 3, 1925.
Chester County Daily Times. December 19, 1960.
Des-Moines Daily News. December 16, 1899.
Fairbanks Daily News Miner. April 21, 1932.
High Point Enterprise. January 17, 1954.
Jefferson Daily Capital News. August 19, 1960.
Leavenworth Echo. January 23, 1920.
Le-Mars-Globe Post. September 11, 1961.

Marshfield Times. December 9, 1908.
Pittsburg Press. January 4, 1944.
Rhinelander New North. February 6, 1919.
Tryon, Henry. *Fearsome Critters.* Idlewild. 1939.
Washington Citizen. January 29, 1943.
Wisconsin-State-Journal. March 27, 1958.

Bee-Squito
Capital Times. February 20, 1930.
Daily Advertiser. July 6, 1998.
Missoulian. February 16, 1923.
Wisconsin Rapids Daily Tribune. February 2, 1927.

Side-Hill Gouger
Argus Leader. January 26, 1943.
Bangor Daily News. January 11, 1977.
Bismarck Tribune. December 1, 2004.
Corvallis Gazette Times. September 12, 1980.
Edmonton Journal. July 28, 1922.
Edmonton Journal. July 24, 1926.
Helena Independent. July 8, 1920.
Province. August 3, 1968.
Province. February 15, 1931.
Rhinelander Daily News. June 16, 1931.
Rhinelander New North. January 22, 1925.
Thompson Falls Independent Ledger. July 26, 1933.
Washington Post. February 6, 1910.

Hodag
Apps, Jerry. *When the White Pines was Kind" A History of Lumberjacks, Log Drives, and Sawdust Cities in Wisconsin.* Wisconsin Historical Society Press. 2020.
Bemidji Pioneer. June 7, 1900.

Canton Press. June 10, 1892.

Cox, William. *Fearsome Creatures of the Lumberwoods*. Judd &Detweiler. 1910.

Daily Tribune. September 30, 1978.

Dorson, Richard. *Man and Beast in American Comic Legend.* Indiana University Press. 1982.

Edmonds, Michael. *Out of the Northwoods: The Many Lives of Paul Bunyan.* Wisconsin Historical Society Press. 2009.

Kingsport Times. May 2, 1937.

Kortenhof, Kurt. Long Live the Hodag.: The life and legacy of Eugene Simeon Shepard 1854-1923. Hodag Press. 2006.

Nortonville News. July 29, 1892.

Philadelphia Inquirer. March 7, 1897.

Rhinelander New North. October 28, 1893.

Hoop Snake

Brown, Charles E. *Paul Bunyan Natural History.* Wisconsin Historical Society. 1935.

Dorson, Richard. *Man and Beast in American Comic Legend.* Indiana University Press. 1982.

Edwardsville Intelligencer. April 9, 1948.

Forest City Courier. November 3, 1927.

Kenosha News. September 20, 1978.

Whirling Whimpus

Buffalo Evening. April 23, 1919.

Calgary Herald. December 9, 1963.

Greenview Sun. May 14, 1937.

Kingsport Times. May 2, 1937.

New Jersey Home News. April 30, 1937.

Spokesman Review. April 3, 1982.

About the Artist

Rick Fisk is a wildlife photographer featuring bald eagles and a digital illustrator featuring cryptids and the paranormal. Online store and contact information at: www.rickfiskphotos.com

About the Author

Chad Lewis seemed destined to write about lumberjack legends and lore. Born and raised in Eau Claire, Wisconsin, a town nicknamed "Sawdust City" due to all the sawmills that once littered the river-banks. As a grade schooler Chad took school field trips to the local Paul Bunyan Logging Camp Museum to learn about the town's log-ging history. After high school, Chad received his bachelor's and master's degrees from the University of Wisconsin-Stout, a college founded by lumber baron James Huff Stout. With this background it only seems fitting that Chad would scour the Northwoods of America in search of the most unbelievable creatures.

More information about Chad can be found at:

www.chadlewisresearch.com